Texting to Your
Teen's Heart

Jane Dinsmore

WESTBOW
PRESS®
A DIVISION OF THOMAS NELSON
& ZONDERVAN

Scripture quotations are taken from the Holy Bible, New International Version®, NIV®. Copyright © 1973, 1978, 1984, 2011 by Biblica, Inc.™ Used by permission of Zondervan. All rights reserved worldwide.

WestBow Press books may be ordered through booksellers or by contacting:

WestBow Press
A Division of Thomas Nelson & Zondervan
1663 Liberty Drive
Bloomington, IN 47403
www.westbowpress.com
1 (866) 928-1240

ISBN: 978-1-5127-6380-5 (sc)
ISBN: 978-1-5127-6379-9 (e)

Library of Congress Control Number: 2016918878

Print information available on the last page.

WestBow Press rev. date: 1/23/2017

Contents

Preface

a message of
encouragement,
hope, humor or
love

The idea for this book came to me while I was sitting alone on my back deck during my quiet time with the Lord. Each day I spend time with God, praying and reflecting. On this particular morning, I was reading *Jesus Calling*, an inspiring devotional written in an unusual manner: as if Jesus is speaking directly to the reader. After reading from this book I was primed, as it were, to hear from God.

"Jane, when you read from this devotional, you feel my unconditional love and encouragement. Communicate this same message of unconditional love, encouragement, and support to your children, with no strings attached. Communicate it in a way they will hear."

As I considered His words, my mind immediately leaped to a technology so present in the lives of my kids: cell phones. I imagined the power of a few well-written words, communicated to my kids through a text.

My heart began to beat quickly as I felt God's presence so strongly at that moment. I knew I needed to take action immediately

Before I acted, I had to contact my wonderful husband, David, and tell him about this moment. We spoke briefly, and he shared my excitement. He could feel the potential this small idea had to change the lives of families.

As I hung up and looked around our home, I was so grateful for the huge number of motivational and spiritual books that my husband has collected over the years. That minute I needed to compose my first texts to my two kids, I had every resource I would need.

I felt an urgency and excitement about beginning this. I had confidence that if God had put this idea in my heart, He would do great things with it. As someone who rarely had texted and who is technologically challenged, feeling driven to send texts to my kids was surprising, to say the least.

Finally, I could not resist the urgings any longer. I am the last person I know who would feel equipped to write a book. I am a woman of action; I love to ski, play tennis, and hike, not sit at a desk and write. But this book seems to come from God more than it comes from me. He loves to use regular folks to accomplish His plans. I am humbled, grateful, and excited that He would choose me to be a part of His work in the hearts of our kids. I have become convinced that I need to share this message with as many people as possible. I am just a regular mom who loves her kids. I want to inspire them to be the best they can be. If I can do it, you can, too.

Introduction

> Kids go where there is excitement. They stay where there is love.
>
> —Zig Ziglar

*L*et's take a glimpse into an ordinary day in the life of your teen. He or she might wake early, dreading the day ahead, envisioning massive amounts of schoolwork, the high expectations of parents, teachers, coaches, and friends, and his or her commitments to the drama club, sports, music, or other extracurricular activities. A sense of being overwhelmed has taken over before the waffle enters the toaster.

Your teen glances at his or her cell phone to look for a diversion, maybe some indication that the day ahead won't be a disaster. He or she is looking for some fun. Your teen expects that the message on his phone is from a friend. He or she reads the message, and it is from you. You've sent a message of encouragement, hope, humor, or love. It could change the course of your teen's day. At the very least he or she knows that you care about your teen and his or her day.

Congratulations! You just sent your first intentional text message!

This book offers a solution for parents looking to find ways to connect with their busy, technology-focused teens.

Are you struck by how little time you have to build a strong relationship with your teen? Do you want to inject more joy into your relationship? Do you see areas where your teen needs guidance?

Maybe you feel overwhelmed by the many difficult issues facing your family or discouraged by your relationship with your teen.

This book is packed with information that will challenge and motivate you to enhance your relationship with your teen. If you and your teen already have a great relationship, then this will add a new depth of connection. If you and your teen are struggling, you may find that this will completely revolutionize your relationship. You will find tools to help you understand your teen more deeply, and truly revitalize your relationship with only a small investment of time.

I have seen good relationships strengthened, and struggling relationships transformed.

Parents sacrifice daily for their children on multiple fronts. We invest money, time, energy, and love in our children, but often, they don't notice or appreciate those sacrifices. Remarkably, the techniques described in this book require the smallest of investments and generate tremendous returns.

The best way to make your children feel secure is not with big deposits in a bank account, but with little deposits of thoughtfulness and affection in the "love account."
—Zig Ziglar

This book is a tool to guide parents and parent surrogates through the process of dramatically enhancing their connections with their teens through the use of a daily text.

This book includes

- the step-by-step process of crafting effective texts;
- guidance on reflecting on your teen;
- a selection of quotations that will speak to your child's heart on critical subjects;
- inspirational stories of the enormous changes parents have witnessed after utilizing this simple technique; and
- strategies to help you avoid pitfalls.

> Affirming words from moms and dads are like light switches. Speak a word of affirmation at the right moment in a child's life and it's like lighting up a whole roomful of possibilities.
> —Gary Smalley

Parents and Others

This book is not just for parents, though throughout the book I will use the word *parent* as a shorthand for all those who stand in as parents in the lives of kids. Is there a teenager in your life who could benefit from a daily supportive, loving, encouraging text message? Then intentional texting will work for you.

I can easily picture grandparents, uncles, aunts, guardians, coaches, neighbors, friends, and godparents successfully using intentional texting. Anyone who knows a child in need of encouragement can make this commitment and transform the life of a child.

Testimonial from a Grandmother

"*Texting Your Teens* has been a great resource for me! I am "Nana" to five pre-teens and have been texting my twelve-year-old granddaughter for several months. I have used several of Jane's suggestions, and it has been a real joy connecting in a way that teens like. She often texts me back with, "'Thanks, Nana. I love you too." I'm excited to get this going with my other four who have not yet gotten cell phones! Jane's book is full of great ideas to encourage our teens. I highly recommend it!"

Texting and Our Kids

**When you put faith, hope, and love together, you
can raise positive kids in a negative world.
—Zig Ziglar**

Texting is the main avenue of communication for youth today. Communicating via text feels natural to them. The impact is high when you join them by communicating with them using texting.

Can you imagine the results if parents harnessed the power of texting and used it to bless, affirm, encourage, and enhance the character of this generation of kids?

Parents today have a strong desire to communicate in a meaningful way with their teens. The power of texting in this context is that it addresses this desire and does so in a way teens are open to receiving.

To illustrate my point, consider the complete focus teens give to reading a text. If parents choose to commit to this process, they have an opportunity to reap the benefits of the intense concentration their teens give to the text messages they receive.

Alternatives to Texting

I recommend that you utilize texting to communicate with your teen; however, if your child prefers e-mails or would respond best to a note in his or her backpack or on the dashboard of his or her car, then that's the best method for you to use. This book will help you craft the right message for your child, and you can choose the most effective delivery system.

If you are like me, you have so much you would like to communicate to your child, but you realize he or she is only available and open to hearing you for a relatively small amount of time. We have to be brief and quick.

Younger Kids

You can easily modify this to use it with your younger kids. The fundamentals of intentional texting will work for all kinds of communication with our kids. Think of the power of a short message from mom tucked inside a backpack or a lunch bag. For the youngest kids it could just be a silly drawing, a smiley face, or a heart. This will convey your love in a profound way and lay the groundwork for the texting you will do once your child is ready for the responsibility of having a phone.

> If kisses were snowflakes, I'd send you a blizzard

Intentional Texting

Intentional texting is a term I use to describe the commitment a parent, guardian, or parent surrogate makes to send a daily text to a child he or she loves with the intention of communicating something purposeful.

> Trust in the Lord with all your heart   and lean not on your own understanding and in all your ways submit to him,   and he will make your paths straight

I love the word *intentional* in this context. Intentional texting is not a difficult or complicated process, but it is something to be done with care and attention. *Our words matter. They have power.* Do you remember messages of hate or hope from your childhood? Decades later, there are words from my childhood that still ring in my mind. One of the great strengths of intentional texting is that it can be done carefully. Some of the conversations we have with our kids quickly spiral out of control

1

into words we wish we could take back. Texting is different. While we are writing a message, we can take our time and craft it carefully.

Intentional texting need not be time-consuming. It will generally be a quick process. Occasionally, our hearts may be burdened to send a message that communicates a subtle or tender subject, and we might take some extra time to choose exactly the right words.

Intentional texting is the perfect addition to the parenting you are already doing. You spend time teaching, disciplining, listening to, and coaching your child. Intentional texting builds on the foundation you have laid with all the time and effort you have put forth.

Finally, intentional texting is a counterbalance to what the modern culture is telling our kids. For example, we might notice that headlines and advertisements glorify the easy life and promote sexuality. We may wish to address this by communicating to our child that hard work is its own reward, modesty is beautiful, or abstinence is not a choice he or she will regret.

Intentional texting is an opportunity to speak truth to our children with care, sensitivity, and kindness.

The Goal of Intentional Texting

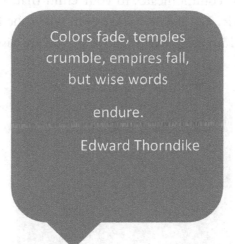

Colors fade, temples crumble, empires fall, but wise words

endure.

Edward Thorndike

I have one underlying goal with intentional texting: I want to communicate to my children, in a way they can hear, how much I love them. Ironically, we don't communicate this best by saying, "I love you," but by taking actions that show them our love. Much of this book is dedicated to helping you pick out the correct words to use with your kids so that the messages you send will inspire them or bring them joy or surprise them with a new way of thinking. However, the main underlying goal is to emphatically let these young men and women know that they are deeply loved.

Each message you send should have the potential to bless, encourage, and build character. In the words that you write is an implicit message that you care. You care enough to notice them and value their individuality and respond to it with a special message. You also care enough to be consistent. This sends children critical messages they are longing to hear: they are valued; we accept them as the people they are; they are important to us; we make them a priority, even on a busy day; we love them deeply; and we want the very best for them.

You will send messages on both easy and difficult days in your relationship. This communicates to your child that, no matter what, you are on his side. You believe in her even when she has lost faith in herself. You love him even when the two of you are disagreeing.

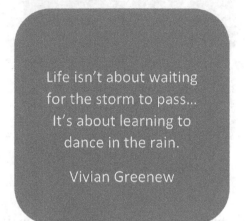

Life isn't about waiting for the storm to pass... It's about learning to dance in the rain.

Vivian Greenew

As sophisticated and knowledgeable as today's teens are, they generally lack the life experience of their parents. When your teen is discouraged or sad, maybe your calm reassurance can transform his or her emotions.

Intentional texting gains power from the fact that the message is individualized to your child. As a parent, you pay close attention to your child. If you think about it for just a moment right now, you probably already know what kind of a message your child would benefit from receiving today. Intentional texting takes the knowledge that you already have and gives you an outlet for expressing to your child what you know he or she needs to hear on a particular day. Note, too, that with the information I share in this book, your understanding of your child will increase without any additional effort expended on your part.

Can you imagine the impact on you if you were to get an affirming or thought-provoking message daily from someone you love? This is what you are providing for your child.

My First Week of Texting

The reality is, we have limited conversation time with our kids. I have a sixteen-year-old son and a fourteen-year-old daughter at home. On any given day, our conversation time is extremely limited. I've seen that texting a daily message lays the groundwork for meaningful communication during the little face-to-face time we do have. Our relationships are being strengthened one brief message at a time.

> Success isn't given. It's earned. On the track, on the field, in the gym. With blood, sweat, and the occasional tear.
>
> Dr. Ann Quinn

Each day of my first week of texting, I reflected on my teens and what they would be facing that day. I thought about the potential difficulties and blessings of the day for them. I prayed, asking the Lord for guidance. Then I looked up some quotes and sent the texts. I felt deeply moved and inspired.

The first week of texting was also my son's first week of football camp for his new school. I thought about all the challenges and joys facing him.

As I sat down to compose a text for my son, many words leaped into my mind from the issues he would be facing: focus, leadership, perseverance, teamwork, and commitment.

Here are some of the messages I sent my son that first week:

1. **An uncommon life doesn't happen by accident. It's a result of the choices, action, and commitments we make to God, ourselves, and our team. Have an amazing week! Love, Mom.**

2. **Coach Dungy said, "Focus on things that you want to have happen, not those that you don't want to happen." Have a great day. Love, Mom.**

3. **"To accomplish great things we must not only act, but also dream; not only plan but also believe." Take action! Love, Mom.**

4. **"People are like sticks of dynamite—the power is on the inside and nothing happens until the fuse gets lit." Weston, light the fuse! Love, Mom.**

This same week, I faced a very different situation with my daughter. I felt moved to equip her with a counterbalance to the societal message that focuses on outward beauty. The biblical perspective that God has made her perfectly and wonderfully seemed exactly right.

I also wanted to encourage her to remember that her efforts for others matter to God; they have eternal significance.

Here are some of the texts I sent my daughter that first week:

1. **"A smile is the light on your face that lets someone know you are home." I love your smile. Love, Mom.**

2. **"Desire what matters to God more than what matters to others." I am so proud to have you as my daughter. Love, Mom.**

3. **Mother Teresa said, "We can do no great things, only small things with great love." Thanks for all you do. Love, Mom.**

One day it had gotten pretty late before I sent my daughter her text. I addressed this in the closing of the text. Here is the text I sent:

"You may not remember what someone does or says, but you will remember how they made you feel." Better late than never. Love, Mom.

As the days passed, I continued to text. I could tell it was paying big dividends in our family relationships. Then I shared what was happening with friends and extended family. The idea captured the imagination of everyone with whom I shared it. They had a lot of questions. They wanted to do what I was doing and to get the results I was getting.

Results

The results were consistent and impressive, confirming that this technique absolutely works, sometimes impacting relationships in astonishing ways. I am excited to see what the effect will be years from now. It is my sincere belief that the rewards from this small investment of consistently pouring loving messages into a teen will be momentous.

The surprise for me through this process has been how widespread the benefits have been. Not only have my kids been blessed, but I have been doubly blessed as I share these experiences with friends and family.

> I love you for all that you are, all that you have been and all you are yet to be

Gathering Data

As I texted my kids daily, I watched for results. Over the months of implementing this process in my home, I have kept a journal recording our progress.

I have also shared the idea with countless friends and family who have in turn shared their experiences with me as they implemented intentional texting.

Finally, a focus group provided additional valuable feedback.

Impact on Kids

> My sheep hear my voice, and I know them, and they follow me, And I give unto them eternal life; and they shall never perish, neither shall any man pluck them out of my hand.
>
> John 10:27-28

Kids who receive the texts feel loved and valued, and they learn that their parent understands them and their lives. This is a welcome relief from and a counterbalance against the stress and destructive influences in their daily life.

- They grow in their confidence in their relationship with their parent.
- Their minds become filled with transformational and empowering words.
- They know they are supported both in times of success and in times of failure.
- They feel acceptance.
- They are amazed at the timing and wisdom.

Further, the stability and strength of their relationship with you empower them to withstand temptations and to be less vulnerable to destructive influences. A child who feels accepted may find he or she is less in need of seeking the approval of peers, with all the dangerous behaviors that this can include.

My desire for my own children is that consistently pouring inspirational words into them will protect them from some of the extreme peer pressure they experience. Intentional texting won't keep your kids or my kids from making mistakes! My kids have made and will make mistakes. Perhaps, though, their growing sense of what kind of people they are and that they are loved will redirect their steps as they are faced with decisions large and small. When they do make mistakes, the pattern of your consistent texting will have taught them that you will be there supporting them no matter what.

I have been careful not to question my own kids too much about their reactions to the texting. Weston said, "It's cool," and Angelina said, "Yeah, I like it," that first week I was texting them. I also overheard them ask each other, "Have you received your message from Mom today?" I love that they are anticipating getting my message.

They did also reveal that after I had started texting, they realized that I care about them and the challenges they are facing each day. Thirty days into the texting, my husband asked the kids, "What do you think of Mom's messages she's been sending you?" My daughter said, "We realize Mom knows what's going on in our lives," and my son chimed in, "And she cares." I was moved to realize they were receiving the underlying message I most wanted them to get: they are loved.

Over time so many other benefits may present themselves. As you focus on your child and craft individualized messages, your insights will help your child to discover his or her own identity and values. This kind of personal knowledge can be life-changing.

> "Life is like a roller coaster. It has its ups and downs. But it's your choice to scream or enjoy the ride."
>
> Michael Rodriguez

Intentional Texting in Action—One Example

Our kids are desperate for this kind of positive interaction with us. When I was speaking with a friend of mine about the intentional texting I was doing, I was very surprised by the response of her daughter who overheard our conversation.

The daughter immediately piped up, "Mom, I want you to do what Mrs. D. is doing with her kids." This young girl so needed this kind of interaction that she asked her mom to do it for her.

One week later, this daughter was posting one of her mom's intentional texts to her Facebook page and writing, "I have the best mom in the world."

Impact on the Writers of the Messages

The impact of this process on me has been a wonderful surprise. My motive was to bless my kids, and through the process, I have been extraordinarily blessed.

The process of selecting and typing inspirational words benefits me, too. These powerful words that I am choosing for my kids work in my own heart throughout the day. I feel the transformative work these words are accomplishing in me. I am often moved to share them with others as well—my husband and my friends.

I feel such a sense of accomplishment in pouring something beneficial into my kids. Scripture calls us to teach our children. We understand the responsibility we have to raise our children well. For years I've yearned to make these kinds of deposits in my kids. I feel a deep satisfaction in daily reaching out to them this way.

Also, the improved connection my kids feel with me has greatly enhanced so much the time we spend together.

Effectiveness of Intentional Texting

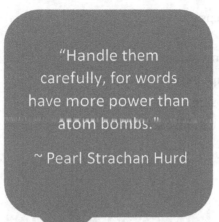

"Handle them carefully, for words have more power than atom bombs."

~ Pearl Strachan Hurd

I believe there is power stored inside great words of wisdom. We transform our minds when we contemplate or meditate on Scripture or other substantive quotations. When my kids get these texts, the powerful words are planted in their brain. They can't help but wonder, "Why did Mom pick this quote for me?" or think about how it applies personally to them. As they tussle, no matter how briefly, with the meanings of the deep messages, they change the direction of their thoughts.

The intrinsic power of these words, coupled with the reflection I've done to help me choose the right message for a particular day, work profoundly in their lives.

Of course, I don't send weighty messages every day. Some of the messages I send are light and silly, intended to make my child laugh and feel joy. These messages work powerfully, too. They express my love and enjoyment of my kids and lighten their moods. They also lay the groundwork for messages of greater significance.

Constructing an Intentional Text Four Steps

There are four steps:

- Reflect on your child today.
- Find an appropriate quotation.
- Add a closing.
- Type the text and send!

> Your talent is God's gift to you. What you do with it is your gift back to God.
>
> Leo Buscaglia

Reflection

As an involved parent, you possess a built-in radar as it relates to your kids. Even if your child hasn't openly revealed what is happening in his or her life, often your gut will tell you when your child is struggling with something. These insights will help you zero in on the type of message you need to send.

During this first step of reflection, you may wish to pray, asking for God's guidance in writing this message.

Reflection Prompts

Here is a list of questions intended to prompt deeper reflection on your teen or give you ideas of what you might need to focus on right now with your communication with your teen:

- What does he or she love to do?
- What makes your teen laugh?
- What is happening in his or her life today, this week, this month?
- What is giving your teen joy today?
- What is making him or her sad?
- Is anything a source of anger?
- Is your teen taking care of himself or herself right now? (Consider your teen's exercise, diet, and sleep habits)?
- Has he or she had some huge successes or spectacular failures?
- Is everything going well right now?
- Are there stresses at home?
- Is your teen overcommitted?
- How is he or she managing all of his or her commitments?
- Has school changed for your teen?
- Does he or she have friends?
- How are your teen's relationships with his or her friends going? Is there a new friend in his or her life?
- Are there sexual pressures in a romantic relationship or your teen's peer group?
- Is he or she being pressured to drink?
- Are there any indications your teen is being bullied?
- Is there particular stress around schoolwork, sports, or extracurricular activities right now?
- Do you see signs he or she is or is not comfortable with how he or she looks?

- Have you seen any evidence of cutting?
- Do you notice any changes in your teen's relationship with food?
- Is he or she always truthful (and if not, what is your teen being deceptive about)?
- How confident is he or she in his or her abilities?
- What is your teen's greatest strength?
- Is there the possibility of being bullied?

As you consider the issues raised by these questions, you may realize that your teen is facing some serious issues that require the help of a professional. As parents, we need to recognize when we need outside help.

Quotation

There are a lot of books on the market to help you choose just the right quote to use for your teen. It is handy to have a book nearby, or you may simply use the Internet to search for a variety of topics.

As time goes by, you may find yourself collecting quotes to use later. When you hear or see something that you think applies well to your teen, it is so easy to collect it for a future message.

Scripture is an abundant and precious resource of quotes. In a later section, I give a little detail about the power of personalizing scripture to an individual. This is a potent technique you will definitely want to employ if you are open to sharing scripture with your child.

A quick search on the Internet will give you access to thousands of additional quotes. Searching by topic and the word *quotation* has yielded great results for me.

You don't need to always use a quotation from someone else. Use your own words on some days. I give examples of some of the messages I've written myself and used with my kids later in the book.

Choosing Quotations

Inject some variety into your texts. Occasionally surprising your teen will keep the interest sparked for both of you.

Humor is a great tool for you to use. It is ok to be light-hearted! I've sent this one: **"Love does not make the world go round; it makes the ride worthwhile."**

Another fun idea is to search for quotes from some of their heroes. Maybe they have a favorite sports hero, or they are drawn to a particular historical figure. Words from someone they already admire will have a deep significance to your teen.

On a particular day, you may send a special message that comes just from you. For example, on our son's sixteenth birthday I sent this (lengthier than usual) message: **"I know without a doubt that the last sixteen years as your mom have blessed me. Embrace the future! You are a young man now. Be all that God made you to be. Inspire those around you. Be unwavering in your faith and you will be greatly blessed. Love, Mom."**

Closing

> Prayer should be the key of the day and the lock of the night.
>
> George Herbert

To conclude your message, you will add a closing sentence that will personalize the message. This is a super simple part, but it may be the most important! Our kids pay close attention to our words. I write a few words letting them know I love them or why I picked this quotation. Then I add the word *Mom* as a "signature" to reinforce that they got this from me. Here are some examples:

> Got your back.—Mom
> Love you!—Mom
> This made me think of you and smile.—Mom
> I'm so proud of you.—Mom
> You are the best!—Mom

The Act of Sending

Finally, you simply send the message. You might pray, "Lord, let this message be a blessing to my child today."

You are finished for today.

Dos and Don'ts of Texting Your Teen

> A gentle answer turns away wrath,
>
> but a harsh word stirs up anger.
>
> Proverbs 15:1

For intentional texting to be most effective, you must be disciplined and send only positive messages. Even though this will be difficult, you must refrain from ever texting a criticism, a lecture, or a harsh judgment.

Be sensitive to your teen's insecurities and vulnerabilities. We've all read a note or e-mail that the sender thought was clever but that was painful to us. Avoid texting teasing remarks or texting on subjects about which your teen is sensitive.

If you casually send a message that ends up hurting your teen, you will obviously damage your relationship, and you may undermine this strategy for the future. It's so easy for your teen to delete your texts without reading them if they have been destructive rather than a blessing.

Steven Covey created a metaphor called an "emotional bank account." Utilizing his concept that positive interactions build up the emotional bank account between two people and negative interactions deplete it, only use intentional texting to build up the emotional bank account you have with your teen.

This concept is more fully described in Covey's book *The Seven Habits of Highly Effective People*.

Do Your Best

I really want to send a truly inspiring, spot-on message every day—one that really pumps them up or helps them or lightens their loads. This has not always happened. But I grant myself grace and persevere.

I continue to believe that this is one of the most rewarding investments I have made for my kids. The trajectory of our relationships has changed because I made this choice. I can't imagine all we would have missed out on if I hadn't done this. I'm so grateful for this idea and how God has used it in my family.

Do Send Message in Times of Conflict

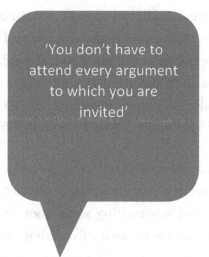

'You don't have to attend every argument to which you are invited'

This is a real challenge. Early on in this process, I had a day of arguments with my son. It was not easy to send a kind, inspirational message, but I knew I needed to do it. I made a decision that we would work out the argument in another way and at another time. I realized I needed to keep the texts separate from any struggles we were having.

Intentional Texting is a gift you are giving your child. Something powerful happens when you choose to continue to lovingly give this gift daily even in the midst of strife with a child. Your child will learn experientially that your love isn't fickle. Your love isn't dependent upon their perfect behavior. You simply love them.

The messages you send may indirectly help bridge the disagreements, and may bring you to reconciliation more quickly.

Testimonial from a Mom

I started intentionally texting my sixteen-and-a-half-year-old son about two months ago. I started with some light, funny quotes or photos. About three days into it, he texted back, "Mom, what's up with the texting stuff. Is your small group doing something about connecting with teens?" He noticed. And I kept doing it.

By the end of the first week of texting, we had encountered one of those really tough patches in the teen-parenting years. Our son was making some poor choices. The timing of those events with this texting project could not have been better. I had the opportunity to send him texts that spoke volumes more than I could say in person. My favorite one during that time was "A lie may take care of the present, but it has no future." I always added a personal sentence or two after the quote or photo. And I always signed it, "Love, Mom." Some days he would write me back with a short response and some days he didn't say a thing. But he would occasionally reference a text/quote that I had sent him weeks before. So they were obviously making a difference.

During this time, my son lost the privilege of using his cell phone. I didn't let that stop the messaging to him. I switched to index cards. I left them in his room, at his desk, in his car, in his bathroom, etc. I soon started noticing that they were being collected in one place on his nightstand. He saved them! One day I even found one of my scripture notecards on his mirror (I didn't put it there—he did). These messages from me as his mother were making an impact.

I feel like this "experiment" happened at just the right time for my son and me. Connecting with him as a teen has gotten a bit harder in the past few years. He connects more easily with my husband. The texting has given me a new way to communicate with him, a new touchpoint for us. I am always paying attention now to things he likes, things he finds funny, interests he has, problems he's going through, or just anything that could influence my new texting connection with him (even really silly stuff that doesn't have a big life lesson attached to it). I have gotten to know him in a different way. I have been able to extend grace via a text when I just couldn't do it in person. I have let him see a new side of me, like sharing some edgy humor. It has forced me to look at his life in a renewed way. And I plan to continue this with him and my other children as they get older. I see so much benefit in it.

Thanks, Jane, for introducing the idea to us. It is helping my relationships! Here are a few of my favorite quotes in case you're looking for some. I don't know all of the authors, though:

"So there's this boy. He kind of stole my heart. He calls me 'Mom.'"

"Poetry is when an emotion has found its thought, and the thought has found words." (He loves writing poetry.)

"Son, you outgrew my lap but never my heart."

"Kindness is a gift everyone can afford to give."

"Never give up on something you can't go a day without thinking about."

"A true test of character isn't how you are on your best days but how you act on your worst days."

Discouragement

Never throw in the towel
use it to wipe off the
sweat and keep going

Having moments of discouragement is completely normal. On busy days it can be a challenge to find even the few minutes it takes to complete the act of sending a text.

When you are not getting positive feedback, or maybe getting no feedback at all, perhaps it will help to remember that you have a small window of opportunity to strengthen your connection with your kids. The day will come when your relationship will be different. You won't be texting them daily. You might wish then that you could. Grab this moment! Choose to persevere.

Even when I'm not getting positive feedback, I choose to continue, trusting that God will bless this effort, today and in the future.

No Time or Little Time to Text

There was one brief period of time in which I simply could not find even a few minutes a day to text my kids.

We had one supertough month. My eighty-six-year-old mother-in-law came to live with us. Unfortunately, her health is not good. She was suffering from confusion and in need of full-time care. Between working, my activities and commitments, and caring for her, I was overwhelmed. I stopped texting.

This was eye-opening to me. I learned how much I missed doing this for my kids. They missed receiving my texts, but truthfully, I think I missed sending them even more. It was a relief to get back to our daily routine of texting.

For particularly busy times, I did make a discovery that helped me to shorten the amount of time my texts took. The shortcut is that it is quicker for me if I settle on a single big idea for my kids for the week and then pull together some quotes ahead of time. For example, I might think about how precious and loved my kids are. Then I would do a quick search and make a list of some quotes that I want to use. Having the quotes already gathered made the process of sending the texts throughout the week even easier. This has been great to do when I know I am facing a busy week.

Don't Expect a Response from Your Teen

Unfortunately, you should not expect to get a response from your teen. You will probably be encouraged at some point by something your teen says to you or says to someone else that gets back to you, but you cannot count on this kind of feedback.

If your child senses that you expect a return text, a thank-you, or some acknowledgment, then the text has become a burden instead of a blessing. There are no strings attached to your texting. You don't want to add to their to-do lists.

It is important not to let your feelings get hurt by a lack of response. This is something you are doing for this child you love. You are doing it unselfishly. This is about doing what is best for your child.

My personal experience is that you will occasionally hear from your child that the texts motivate him or her, make your teen laugh, help him or her to focus or see something more clearly, etc. You might hear that it makes them feel loved. Sometimes the kids enjoy the texts so much they forward them on to their friends or put them in a paper they are writing for school. You may or may not ever learn about that.

Incorporating Scripture into Texts

> For God hath not given
> us the spirit of fear; but
> of power, and of love,
> and of a sound mind.
>
> 2 Timothy 1:7

Personalizing passages from the Holy Bible is a powerful technique in texting and in life.

If you haven't done this, it is a simple process of changing the text just a little: inserting a name and if necessary changing the pronouns so that they personally apply to someone. Individuals, while praying or reading scripture, often will personalize the text to apply it to themselves. This is the same idea, now applied to your teen.

Here is a quick example:

> Deuteronomy 4:29 says, "But if from there you seek the Lord your God, you will find him if you look for him with all your heart and with all your soul."

I suggest you only include the words that are helpful to you. In this case, if I was writing this to my daughter, I might write, **"Angelina, seek the Lord your God with all your heart and with all your soul, and you will find Him."**

The promises of God are published in many forms and can be searched for on the Internet. You may already have a promise Bible in your home. If so, you may wish to fish it out and try individualizing those promises and claiming them for you and for your teen.

It is ok to paraphrase the passage or use a different translation than you usually use in order to make this fit your situation well. BibleGateway. com is a great, free resource where it is easy to quickly search by topic and then sample a bunch of different translations to find one that works best. I love the NIV and the King James versions for Bible study, and The Message is often a great choice.

Intentional Texting—Going Deeper

> Parents can only give good advice or put them on the right path, the final forming of a person's character lies in their own hands.
> **Anne Frank**

ou may find you want to challenge your child in an even deeper way with your texts. In this implementation of intentional texting, you consider the character traits of your child, and among the messages you send, you include some messages that will help them to become young men and young women with strong character.

There is little that matters as much as their character. Integrity, kindness, courage, wisdom, empathy, patience, honesty, respectfulness, responsibility, and fairness are great examples of the traits we wish for our kids, but we may wonder how to help them develop.

I suggest that we can encourage the development of these traits through our texts. We may want to choose subtle rather than overt messages for this.

We may find we often rely on humor with these messages.

Below I've listed some character traits and some questions relating to each trait. These may raise some areas you feel could be addressed well through a text.

Issues Facing Teen's today

I've compiled a list of some issues facing teens today. Your teen may be:

- balancing work and play,
- persevering in the face of difficulty,
- gracefully responding to success and failure,
- choosing school and career paths,
- navigating difficult relationships,
- facing isolating circumstances,
- coping with loss,
- forming a sense of his identity, or
- taking a stand for what he believes in.

Your text can powerfully influence your teen in the midst of these and other challenging circumstances. Your text can send the message that his or her choices matter and that he or she is not alone.

Consider Your Teen's Personality

Regardless of your teen's personality traits, he or she will benefit from intentional texting.

Your teen may be bold, outspoken, and strong-willed; thoughtful, introspective, and focused; imaginative and innovative; or adventuresome.

You will want to consider your teen's personality and choose messages that further develop strengths and help to overcome weaknesses. Considering your teen's unique characteristics will help you to touch his or her heart.

Some Character Traits

Accountability—Does your teen admit it when he or she makes a mistake? Can he or she say, "I messed up"?

Caring—Does your child notice what other people are going through, and does it move him or her to action?

Confidence—Does your teen accurately see his or her strengths, talents, and abilities? Does he or she know it is ok to try something and fail? Would he or she feel able to protest situations your teen felt were wrong?

Courage—How does your teen respond to difficult challenges? Will fear hold him or her back?

Diligence—Does he or she persevere through a task that requires a sustained effort?

Discernment—Does your teen accurately assess situations?

Empathy—Does your child need prompting to consider another's circumstances? Does this come very naturally to him or her?

Forgiveness—Does your teen easily forgive those who have wronged him or her?

Friendship—How highly does your child value his or her relationships? Does he or she have healthy boundaries?

Generosity—Has your teen learned the joy of giving?

Honesty—Does your teen bend the truth?

Humility—Is your teen enjoying great success? How is he or she coping with success?

Joyfulness—Does he or she have an underlying joy independent of his or her circumstances?

Leadership—Is your teen a good example for other kids? Does he or she step into leadership roles? Is your teen a good follower?

Loyalty—Is he or she consistent in his or her loyalties? Is your child a reliable friend?

Peacefulness—Is your teen able to compromise and cooperate with others? Does a change in circumstances "throw" him or her, or does your child maintain his or her calm?

Purity—Is your teen morally excellent?

Purposeful—Does your child have a skill, talent, or interest that he or she wants to develop?

Respect—Does your teen regard everyone as being worthy of his or her respect?

Responsibility—Is your teen great at following through with his or her commitments?

Righteousness—Is your teen in good standing with God?

Wisdom—Does he or she have good instincts and an ability to apply his or her knowledge and experience to a new set of circumstances?

It Is Time for You to Send Your First Intentional Text

Reflect on your child and the day he or she is facing. As time goes by, you will be observing your child more intently than before, and you will increasingly understand your child. On this first day, simply trust your instincts about your child and hone in on what kind of a message you want to send.

Find your quote using some of the ideas listed here.

Type or copy the quote with an uplifting closing and your name.

Send.

Final Thoughts

The most important step is for you to make a commitment to write and send your child a personalized message each day.

I pray God's great blessings on you and your family as you begin this process. I pray that intentional texting will powerfully enhance your relationships and infuse them with joy. Finally, I pray the impact will be lasting and deep and beyond your wildest expectations.

Acknowledgements

S itting down to write a book has never been one of my goals. I share in the book how this process started and am so thankful to God for granting this small miracle.

I would like to thank all my friends, family and clients who took the time to read the book in the early stages and encourage me to continue with the idea.

I would like to thank Sara Leing for her excitement and encouragement in the beginning stages of the editing process.

I would like to thank my nephew Travis whose creative art talent contributed to the initial design of the cover and the idea to use the interior bubble quote images.

I am so very thankful to my husband David and the children who were my willing subjects of my messages. The children let me know how inspired and challenged they felt and most importantly they let me know that they knew I loved them. ♥♥♥

About the Author

*J*ane is a loving wife, a busy and fun mother of four (with two teens at home), a devoted Christian, a longtime hair stylist of many, and an adventurer on the Colorado Ski Mountain. Writing, typing, and authoring a book has never crossed her mind. The idea for this book came on a routine quiet morning with the Lord. One keystroke at a time, and now you hold the finished product.

Printed in the United States
By Bookmasters